SUMMARY OF THEOLOGY SIMPLIFIED

2

The Eight Foundational Truths for Understanding God's Plan for Man

BOB YANDIAN

Copyright 2024–Harrison House

All rights reserved. This book is protected by the copyright laws of the United States of America. This book may not be copied or reprinted for commercial gain or profit. The use of short quotations or occasional page copying for personal or group study is permitted and encouraged. Permission will be granted upon request. Unless otherwise indicated, all scripture quotations are taken from the *King James Version* of the Bible. Used by permission. All rights reserved.

All emphasis within Scripture quotations is the author's own. Please note that Harrison House's publishing style capitalizes certain pronouns in Scripture that refer to the Father, Son, and Holy Spirit, and may differ from some publishers' styles. Take note that the name satan and related names are not capitalized. We choose not to acknowledge him, even to the point of violating grammatical rules.

Harrison House P.O. Box 310, Shippensburg, PA 17257-0310

This book and all other Harrison House's books are available at Christian bookstores and distributors worldwide.

For Worldwide Distribution.

Reach us on the Internet: www.harrisonhouse.com.

ISBN 13 TP: 9781667508115

ISBN 13 eBook: 9781667508122

CONTENTS

Introduction   v

1. The Doctrine of Theology: A Study of the Person of God   1
2. The Doctrine of the Fall of Man: A Study of the Tree of the Knowledge of Good and Evil   5
3. The Doctrine of Faith for Salvation: A Study of the Only Means of Redemption   9
4. The Doctrine of Unlimited Atonement   13
5. The Doctrine of Advocacy   17
6. The Doctrine of Dispensations and Times   21
7. The Doctrine of the Church   25
8. The Doctrine of Two Books: Life and Works   29

About the Publisher   33

INTRODUCTION

Welcome to the condensed exploration of "Theology Simplified 2," a comprehensive guide designed to demystify complex theological concepts and present them in an accessible manner. This summary distills the key teachings and insights from the book, aiming to provide a clear and succinct understanding of fundamental theological principles. Whether you are a student of theology, a spiritual seeker, or simply curious about the deeper questions of faith, this summary will offer you valuable insights and a clearer understanding of the intricate world of theological study. We will navigate through the essential doctrines, historical contexts, and spiritual implications that define and shape the Christian faith. Join us as we uncover the profound depths of theological inquiry, simplified for everyday understanding and practical application.

CHAPTER 1

THE DOCTRINE OF THEOLOGY: A STUDY OF THE PERSON OF GOD

Bible Verse

Romans 11:33-36 - "Oh, the depth of the riches both of the wisdom and knowledge of God! How unsearchable are His judgments and His ways past finding out!"

Introduction

Exploring the nature and character of God poses a profound challenge due to the vast disparity between human limitations and God's infinite qualities. This chapter delves into the complexities of understanding an eternal, perfect being from our finite, imperfect perspective.

Word of Wisdom

"We will never fully understand God, probably not even into eternity." - A candid acknowledgment of our perpetual

quest to comprehend the divine. Bob Yandian

Main Theme

The main theme of this chapter revolves around the inherent difficulties humans face in attempting to study and understand the infinite attributes of God, using scriptural insights and theological reflections to guide us.

Key Points

- Understanding God is inherently challenging due to His infinite nature contrasted with our finite existence.
- Scripture is our primary tool for gaining insight into God's character and attributes.
- The Trinity exemplifies God's complex unity as three distinct persons working harmoniously.
- Jesus Christ provides a tangible connection to understanding the divine through His life and teachings.
- The concept of God's perfect plan encompasses creation and redemption, designed perfectly despite humanity's imperfections.
- Our response to God's offer of salvation through Jesus Christ determines our eternal destiny.

Key Themes

- **God's Unsearchable Nature:** Human beings struggle to grasp the full extent of God's wisdom and knowledge, as our tools and language are insufficient to fully articulate His attributes.
- **The Role of Scripture:** The Bible serves as a vital resource, allowing us to explore aspects of God's character such as His eternal nature, sovereignty, and love, albeit within the limitations of human understanding.
- **Insight into the Trinity:** The doctrine of the Trinity showcases the unique yet unified roles of the Father, Son, and Holy Spirit, providing a foundational aspect of Christian theology that reflects on the unity and diversity within God's nature.
- **Jesus as the Revelation of God:** Jesus is portrayed as the visible image of the invisible God, whose actions and words on earth provide clear insights into the nature of God the Father.
- **The Perfect Divine Plan:** Despite humanity's flawed nature, God's redemption plan through Christ is perfect, underscoring His ability to work through imperfect beings to fulfill His divine purposes.
- **Human Responsibility in Salvation:** The chapter emphasizes the individual's choice in accepting or rejecting Jesus Christ, highlighting the personal responsibility we hold in our relationship with God.

Conclusion

The chapter concludes with a poignant reflection on the eternal journey of discovering God's infinite nature. It suggests that even with eternal life and a perfect resurrection body, humanity will continue to explore the inexhaustible attributes of God, continually growing in understanding but never fully comprehending His entirety. This exploration is both a humbling and exalting aspect of the Christian faith.

CHAPTER 2

THE DOCTRINE OF THE FALL OF MAN: A STUDY OF THE TREE OF THE KNOWLEDGE OF GOOD AND EVIL

Bible Verse

Romans 5:12 - "Therefore, just as through one man sin entered the world, and death through sin, and thus death spread to all men, because all sinned."

Introduction

This chapter examines the pivotal event of humanity's fall through Adam's disobedience at the Tree of the Knowledge of Good and Evil, emphasizing its enduring impact on all of humanity and contrasting it with the redemptive act of Christ on the cross.

Word of Wisdom

"Since we were in Adam at the time, we fell with him. Adam's fall included us. We did not choose to be born into sin. Adam chose for us." Bob Yandian

Main Theme

The chapter explores the theological concept of original sin, introduced through Adam's disobedience, its consequences for humanity, and the redemption available through Jesus Christ, the "Last Adam," who provides a path from death to life.

Key Points

- Humanity's inherent sinfulness stems from Adam's choice, not individual transgressions.
- The Tree of the Knowledge of Good and Evil symbolizes the introduction of sin into the world.
- Christ's crucifixion on the cross represents the antithesis of Adam's act, offering salvation and life.
- Every human is spiritually connected to either Adam's fall or Christ's redemption.
- The nature of sin, embedded in human flesh, can only be overcome through spiritual rebirth in Christ.
- Choices made by individuals continue to determine their spiritual life and eternal destiny.

Key Themes

- **Impact of Adam's Disobedience:**
Adam's decision to eat from the forbidden tree brought sin and death into the world, affecting all his descendants. This foundational act of disobedience illustrates

the profound consequences of a single act of rebellion against God.
- **Symbolic Significance of Trees:** The trees in the Garden of Eden—the Tree of Life and the Tree of the Knowledge of Good and Evil—symbolize life and death, respectively. The choices made by Adam and Eve at these trees have eternal implications for all of humanity.
- **Redemption Through Christ:** Jesus Christ, referred to as the Last Adam, contrasts with the first Adam by obeying God completely and sacrificing Himself on the cross. His act of obedience provides the only effective remedy for the curse of sin introduced by Adam.
- **Inherent Sin and Human Nature:** The nature of sin is deeply ingrained in human flesh and is passed down through generations. This inherent sin can only be overcome through spiritual regeneration, which is made possible by Christ's atonement.
- **The Role of Individual Choice in Salvation:** While Adam's choice affects all humanity, each person has the opportunity to choose Christ and move from the lineage of Adam to the lineage of Christ, thereby changing their eternal destiny.

Conclusion

The doctrine of the fall of man underscores the severity of Adam's sin and its extensive consequences for humanity, juxtaposed with the hope and redemption offered through Jesus Christ. By choosing to align with Christ rather than Adam, individuals can escape the legacy of sin and embrace eternal life. This chapter provides a foundational understanding of original sin and redemption, emphasizing the transformative power of individual choice in the face of inherited sin.

CHAPTER 3

THE DOCTRINE OF FAITH FOR SALVATION: A STUDY OF THE ONLY MEANS OF REDEMPTION

Bible Verse

Ephesians 2:8-9 - "For by grace you have been saved through faith, and that not of yourselves; it is the gift of God, not of works, lest anyone should boast."

Introduction

This chapter delves into the consistent biblical theme that faith alone is the means by which humanity can attain salvation, a concept that remains unchanged from the Old Testament to the New Testament. The author challenges common misconceptions about the role of the law and sacrifices in salvation, emphasizing that these were never means to save but were designed to point towards Christ.

Word of Wisdom

"By the deeds of the law no flesh will

be justified in His sight" (Romans 3:20) - reinforcing that salvation is based not on human deeds but on divine grace.

Main Theme

The chapter explores the concept of faith as the sole means for salvation throughout biblical history, clarifying that neither the Mosaic law nor the sacrificial system were ever intended to provide salvation, which comes exclusively through faith in Jesus Christ.

Key Points

- Old Testament saints were saved by faith in God, much like believers today.
- The law was given to reveal human sinfulness and our need for a savior, not as a means of salvation.
- Animal sacrifices highlighted the necessity of a substitutionary atonement, pointing to Jesus' ultimate sacrifice.
- Throughout history, the consistent message of the Bible is that salvation is a gift of grace received through faith.
- The law and sacrifices served as tutors to lead humanity to Christ, demonstrating that salvation cannot be earned.
- Faith in the redemptive work of Christ is the central requirement for salvation,

transcending all dispensations and covenants.

Key Themes

- **Misunderstandings about Salvation:** The chapter begins by addressing common misconceptions among students and believers about how salvation was achieved historically, particularly under the Old Covenant, correcting the view that it was through law observance or sacrifices.
- **Role of the Law and Sacrifices:** The law was intended to make clear the sinfulness of man and our inability to achieve righteousness on our own, serving as a tutor that leads to Christ, who offers justification by faith. Sacrifices were illustrative, pointing to the necessity and sufficiency of Christ's sacrifice for sin.
- **Historical Consistency of Salvation through Faith:** The author emphasizes that from the Old Testament through the New Testament, salvation has consistently been accessible only through faith. This faith was initially in God's promises, which are fully revealed in Jesus Christ.
- **Practical Implications of Salvation by Faith:** By explaining that the law and sacrifices teach us about our sin and need for a savior, the chapter reinforces that true salvation alters one's life, leading to peace and assurance of salvation, which are immediate results of genuine faith.
- **Continuity and Fulfillment in Christ:** The New Testament does not abolish the

teachings of the Old but fulfills them, showing that the rituals and laws were shadows of the reality found in Christ. This fulfillment is central to understanding the purpose and effectiveness of Jesus' redemptive work.

Conclusion

The doctrine of faith for salvation illustrates the unchanging nature of God's plan for humanity's redemption. Despite the different covenants and dispensations, the requirement of faith remains constant, underscoring that salvation is not based on human efforts but on Christ's finished work. This chapter highlights the simplicity and profundity of salvation by faith, encouraging readers to rely wholly on Jesus for their salvation.

CHAPTER 4

THE DOCTRINE OF UNLIMITED ATONEMENT

Bible Verse

1 John 2:2 - "He is the propitiation for our sins, and not for ours only but also for the whole world."

Introduction

This chapter explores the concept of unlimited atonement within Christian theology, arguing against the idea that Christ's atoning sacrifice was limited to a select group of "elect" individuals. It emphasizes the compatibility of divine sovereignty and human free will.

Word of Wisdom

"The Lord is...not willing that any should perish but that all should come to repentance" (2 Peter 3:9).

Main Theme

The main theme focuses on the theological assertion that Jesus Christ's atoning sacrifice was intended for all humanity, not just a predestined few. This unlimited atonement underscores the breadth of God's love and the universal scope of salvation offered through Jesus Christ.

Key Points

• Christ's sacrifice is intended for all, aligning with God's desire for universal salvation.

• The doctrine of unlimited atonement contrasts with limited atonement, which suggests Christ died only for the elect.

• Scripture supports the view that Christ's atonement is universally applicable and effective.

• Human free will allows individuals to accept or reject the salvation offered through Christ.

• The balance of God's sovereignty and human responsibility is crucial in understanding salvation.

Key Themes

- **Theological Balance of Sovereignty and Free Will:** The chapter discusses how God's sovereignty does not negate human free will but rather works in conjunction with it to facilitate salvation. This balance is essential for understanding how divine foreknowledge and human choice coexist without conflict.

- **Biblical Evidence Supporting Unlimited Atonement:** Various scriptures, such as 1 John 2:2 and John 3:16, are cited to affirm that Christ's redemptive work was intended for every individual, thereby supporting the concept of unlimited atonement over against doctrines of limited atonement.
- **Implications for Evangelism and Faith Practice:** The belief in unlimited atonement fuels the Christian mandate for evangelism, encouraging believers to preach the gospel universally, as salvation is potentially available to all people regardless of their background.
- **Historical and Doctrinal Context:** The chapter situates the doctrine of unlimited atonement within the broader historical debates on atonement theory, discussing how it has been variously interpreted and the implications of these interpretations for Christian doctrine and practice.
- **Practical and Pastoral Considerations:** The understanding that atonement is unlimited impacts pastoral care and the theological education of believers, encouraging an inclusive and proactive approach to faith practice and community engagement.

Conclusion

The doctrine of unlimited atonement not only highlights the extent of God's grace but also calls for a responsible Christian response that acknowledges and propagates this universal offer of salvation. It challenges believers to live out their faith with a recognition of God's sovereign grace and to actively participate in the Great Commission, ensuring that the message of Christ's sacrifice reaches every corner of the world.

CHAPTER 5

THE DOCTRINE OF ADVOCACY

Bible Verse

1 John 2:1 - "My little children, these things I write to you, so that you may not sin. And if anyone sins, we have an Advocate with the Father, Jesus Christ the righteous."

Introduction

This chapter explores the concept of advocacy in the spiritual realm, illustrating how believers receive divine support through Jesus Christ, the Holy Spirit, and fellow believers. It emphasizes the ongoing need for this divine assistance throughout the earthly life of a believer.

Word of Wisdom

"If we have sinned and confess our sins, the issue is over immediately, and the case is thrown out of court." Bob Yandian

Main Theme

The theme revolves around the multifaceted support system that God has provided for believers, comprising Jesus Christ, the Holy Spirit, and the Christian community. This divine advocacy addresses our spiritual, legal, and practical needs until we reach heaven.

Key Points

- Advocacy in biblical terms involves strength, assistance, and legal defense provided by Jesus Christ and the Holy Spirit.

- Jesus Christ serves as an advocate for believers, interceding on their behalf for forgiveness and protection.

- The Holy Spirit acts as an advocate by assisting in prayer and supporting believers in their weaknesses.

- Believers are also called to advocate for one another, supporting each other through trials and failures.

- Understanding our divine advocacy helps believers navigate life's challenges with confidence and peace.

Key Themes

- **Dual Advocacy of Christ and the Holy Spirit:** Jesus Christ advocates for us in heaven, handling our sins and accusations from Satan, ensuring they are dismissed when confessed. The Holy Spirit aids us on earth, guiding us in situations where we lack the wisdom or strength to proceed.

- **Comprehensive Divine Assistance:** This advocacy is not just about spiritual warfare or legal defense; it also involves practical guidance through the Holy Spirit in day-to-day life challenges and decisions, emphasizing a holistic approach to divine support.
- **Believers' Role in Advocacy:** Just as Christ and the Holy Spirit advocate for us, we are called to advocate for each other. This involves bearing each other's burdens, restoring those who falter, and using our experiences to aid others in their spiritual journeys.
- **Satan's Role as Accuser:** The chapter details how Satan functions as the accuser, presenting believers' sins before God. However, Jesus' advocacy effectively counters all accusations, as He confirms that all confessed sins have been paid for on the cross.
- **Eternal and Temporal Implications:** While the advocacy of Jesus and the Holy Spirit has eternal implications for our salvation and standing before God, it also has temporal benefits, providing peace and practical help throughout our lives on earth.

Conclusion

The doctrine of advocacy is central to understanding the full scope of God's provision for His people. By recognizing Jesus Christ and the Holy

Spirit as our advocates, and by engaging in advocacy for one another, believers can navigate life assured of God's active involvement and support in every circumstance. This divine advocacy ensures that believers are never alone in their struggles and are always supported by a powerful spiritual defense and guidance system.

CHAPTER 6

THE DOCTRINE OF DISPENSATIONS AND TIMES

Bible Verse

Hebrews 1:1-2 - "God, who at various times and in various ways spoke in time past to the fathers by the prophets, has in these last days spoken to us by His Son, whom He has appointed heir of all things, through whom also He made the worlds."

Introduction

This chapter delves into the concept of dispensations, defining them as distinct periods or administrations of time, wherein God interacts with humanity in specific ways according to the divine plan. The chapter highlights the uniqueness of the Church Age within this framework.

Word of Wisdom

"The same God, our Father, spoke in the Old Testament and the New Testa-

ment. He spoke in the Old Testament through the prophets. He spoke in the New Testament through Christ, His Son, who spoke through the apostles." Bob Yandian

Main Theme

The primary theme is the exploration of how God's methods of interaction and the responsibilities of mankind have shifted across different dispensations, culminating in the current Church Age, which is marked by a unique interaction through the Holy Spirit and the collective body of Christ.

Key Points

• Dispensations are distinct periods during which God administers his relationship with humanity in specific ways.

• The Church Age is a unique dispensation hidden in the past but revealed in the New Testament as a "mystery."

• Each dispensation begins with divine initiation and ends typically due to human failure.

• There are seven primary dispensations, from the age of innocence to the prophesied millennium.

• The current Church Age is characterized by the indwelling of the Holy Spirit and the unity of Jewish and Gentile believers.

- The Church Age will conclude with the rapture, leading into the tribulation and eventually the millennial reign of Christ.

Key Themes

- **Concept and Purpose of Dispensations:** Dispensations demonstrate God's sovereign administration over history, where each period is initiated by God in response to the spiritual state of humanity, aiming to reveal different aspects of His character and plan for salvation.
- **The Mystery of the Church Age:** The Church Age is described as a mystery that was hidden from previous ages and revealed only in the New Testament. It represents a period where the barrier between Jew and Gentile is abolished, and all believers are united under one body through Christ.
- **Transition Between Dispensations:** The transitions between dispensations are critical moments where God's dealings with humanity shift in response to human actions, demonstrating a balance of divine judgment and mercy.
- **The Role of the Church in the Current Dispensation:** The Church is tasked with spreading the Gospel and demonstrating the kingdom of God on Earth, empowered by the Holy Spirit to fulfill roles and ministries that continue the work of Christ.

- **Fulfillment of Prophecies and Promises:** Each dispensation fulfills specific biblical prophecies and promises, with the Church Age fulfilling the mystery of the Gentiles and Jews sharing in the promises of Christ's redemptive work.

Conclusion

The doctrine of dispensations provides a framework for understanding the historical and future plans of God as revealed through scripture. The current Church Age holds a special place in this plan, serving as a precursor to the final dispensation of the millennium. Believers are called to appreciate the uniqueness of this age and live in a manner that honors the responsibilities it entails, actively participating in the global mission of the Church while awaiting Christ's return.

CHAPTER 7

THE DOCTRINE OF THE CHURCH

Bible Verse
Matthew 16:18 - "I will build My church, and the gates of Hades shall not prevail against it."

Introduction

This chapter explores the concept of the Church in the New Testament, distinguishing between the universal Church and local church congregations. It discusses the origins, purpose, and operational dynamics of the Church from its inception on the Day of Pentecost to its function and significance in the lives of believers.

Word of Wisdom

"Jesus builds the true Church, adds people as they are saved, and multiplies the numbers who come." Bob Yandian

Main Theme

The dual nature of the Church as both a universal body encompassing all believers and localized congregations that meet regularly, highlighting the role of the Church in fostering spiritual growth and community among Christians.

Key Points

• The Church began on the Day of Pentecost, establishing both the universal Church and the first local church.

• The Greek term "ekklesia," translated as church, literally means "called out ones," emphasizing believers called out from the world.

• Local churches serve as visible representations of the universal Church, focusing on discipleship and community.

• The concept of the Church encompasses a two-thousand-year period known as the Church Age.

• Local churches are not defined by their buildings but by the congregating believers within.

Key Themes

- **Theological Foundations and Functions:** The Church is fundamentally a community of believers globally (universal) and locally, called to live out the teachings of Jesus Christ and support one another in spiritual growth. This calling

defines both the purpose and the operational essence of the Church.
- **Distinctiveness of the Church in God's Plan:** Unlike any other institution, the Church is designed by God to be the manifestation of His kingdom on Earth through the lives of believers, tasked with the mission of evangelism and spiritual edification.
- **Role of Local Churches:** Local churches are essential for providing believers with spiritual nourishment through teaching, fellowship, and communal worship. They play a critical role in manifesting the universal Church's presence worldwide.
- **Leadership and Growth:** Jesus Christ is depicted as the ultimate builder of the Church, emphasizing that the growth and sustenance of both universal and local churches depend on divine rather than human leadership.
- **Ecclesiastical Identity and Community Impact:** The Church's identity as a community of believers transcends cultural, racial, and social divisions, promoting a unified identity in Christ which should be reflected in the inclusive nature of local church communities.

Conclusion

The Church, as described in the New Testament, operates both universally and locally to fulfill Christ's commission. It serves as a spiritual home for believers, providing a platform for worship, learning, and communal support, all while underpinning the broader mission of spreading the Gospel. The Church remains central to God's plan for humanity, serving as a beacon of hope and a source of renewal for believers worldwide.

CHAPTER 8

THE DOCTRINE OF TWO BOOKS: LIFE AND WORKS

Bible Verse

Revelation 20:12 - "And I saw the dead, small and great, standing before God, and books were opened. Another book was opened, which is the Book of Life. And the dead were judged according to their works, by the things which were written in the books."

Introduction

This chapter delves into the significant biblical concept of the Book of Life and the Book of Works, exploring how beliefs about these books influence understandings of judgment and salvation, emphasizing the necessity of faith in Jesus for true salvation.

Word of Wisdom

"Only those who accept Jesus as their Savior have reached perfection. They

share Jesus' righteousness and are thus found in the Book of Life." Bob Yandian

Main Theme

The text examines the distinct roles of the Book of Life and the Book of Works in divine judgment, illustrating the futility of relying on one's own deeds for salvation and highlighting the critical importance of having one's name written in the Book of Life through faith in Jesus Christ.

Key Points

• Many people mistakenly believe their good deeds will secure their heavenly admission.

• True salvation is only granted through faith in Jesus Christ, not by personal merit.

• The Book of Works records deeds but does not determine eternal destiny regarding salvation.

• The Book of Life is crucial, as it contains the names of those granted eternal life through Jesus.

• During judgment, the Book of Works proves the insufficiency of works for salvation.

• Eternal rewards for believers are determined by deeds recorded in the Book of Works.

Key Themes

- **Misplaced Faith in Works:** Many believe that their good deeds will outweigh their bad, qualifying them for heaven. This chapter clarifies that such belief is misguided, as divine standards require perfection, which only faith in Jesus can impute.

- **Judgment and the Two Books:** The Book of Works serves to show individuals that no amount of good works can achieve the perfection required by God, while the Book of Life lists those who have accepted Christ's sacrifice and are thereby justified.
- **The Role of Jesus in Salvation:** Emphasizing the unique role of Jesus Christ, the discussion outlines that rejecting Jesus is the sole sin leading to damnation, highlighting the necessity of recognizing and accepting Jesus' atonement.
- **Great White Throne Judgment:** This eschatological event is described, where those not found in the Book of Life face the second death. For believers, the focus at judgment is on rewards, not condemnation.
- **Practical Implications for Believers:** The chapter urges believers to live out their faith actively, demonstrating the reality of their salvation through good works, which are evidence of genuine faith but are not the means of salvation.

Conclusion

The chapter asserts that understanding the roles of the Book of Life and the Book of Works is crucial for Christians. It challenges believers to reflect on the source of their confidence for salvation and encourages them to ensure their lives reflect genuine faith through actions inspired by the Holy Spirit, not by self-derived efforts. This teaching aims to secure believers in their faith and motivate them to live righteously, serving as visible testimonies of God's grace.

Harrison House is a Spirit-filled, Word of Faith Christian publisher dedicated to spreading the message of faith, hope, and love through our wide range of inspiring publications. Committed to the messages that highlight the power of the Word and Spirit, we provide books, devotionals, and study guides that empower believers to live victorious, faith-filled lives.

Our resources are designed to help readers grow spiritually, strengthen their faith, and experience the transformative power of God's Word. Harrison House is passionate about equipping Christians with the tools they need to fulfill their divine purpose and impact the world for Christ.